ZAZULEAC WORLD

We hope you have a great experience with this book and we appreciate your support.

Connect With Us:

Love Jar Alphabet

Write the missing lower case letters in the empty jars

a ♡

c d ♡ f g h

♡ j k l ♡ n

♡ p ♡ ♡ s t

♡ v w ♡ y ♡

Numbers

Draw the amount of ♥'s in blank spot of each number

Missing Hearts

Write the missing numbers

Tracing Hearts

Tacing Honey Bee Heart

Trace The Numbers

1	2	3	4
5	6	7	8
9	10	11	12
13	14	15	16
17	18	19	20

Numbers

5

Color it

5

Make it

Find and Color

1 5 2 5
4 15 9 5
5 2 3 5

✎ Trace and Write ✎

5 5 5 5 5

Five

Color 5 cars

Five

Paste it

5 5 1 5 3 5

6

Color it

6

Make it

Find and Color

6 2 2 16
8 20 7 6
6 2 6 6

✎ Trace and Write ✎

6 6 6 6 6

Six

Six

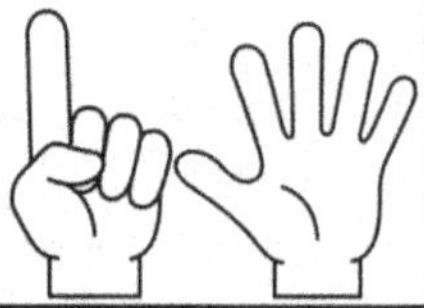

Paste it

11 6 6 1 6 6

7

Color it

7

Make it

Find and Color

4 7 2 17
7 7 8 2
7 5 9 7

✎ Trace and Write ✎

7 7 7 7 7

Seven

Seven

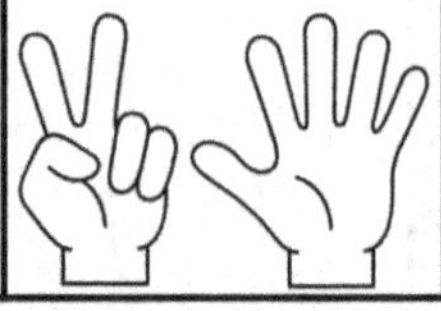

Paste it

7 7 20 7 7 12

8

Color it

8

Make it

Find and Color

9 8 2 8
18 8 11 2
1 8 9 8

✎ Trace and Write ✎

8 8 8 8 8

Eight

Eight

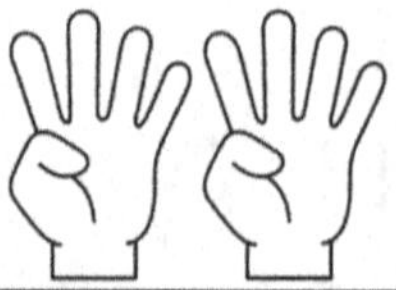

Paste it

14 8 8 2 8 8

Number 9

Color it
9

Make it

Find and Color
19 9 5 9
9 1 11 9
8 9 2 7

Trace and Write

9 9 9 9 9

Nine

	Nine	Paste it

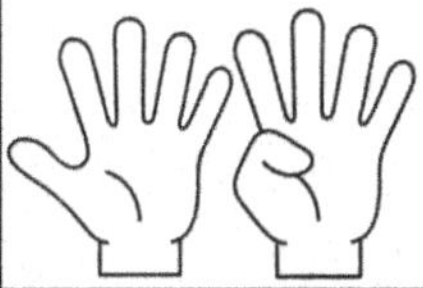

9 10 9 9 7 9

Number 10

Color it
10

Make it

Find and Color
20 7 4 10
1 10 3 9
10 8 5 10

Trace and Write

10 10 10

Ten

	Ten	Paste it

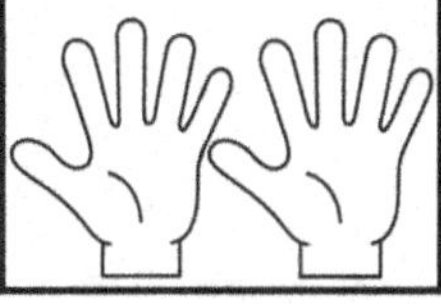

10 5 13 10 10 10

Number 11

Color it
11

Make it

Find and Color
11 8 5 11
8 11 11 6
14 8 11 17

Trace and Write

11 11 11

Eleven

	Eleven	Paste it

8 11 11 2 11 11

Number 12

Color it
12

Make it

Find and Color
9 12 15 12
5 12 10 3
12 7 6 12

Trace and Write

12 12 12

Twelve

	Twelve	Paste it

6 12 9 12 12 12

Color it

13

Make it

Find and Color

11	8	13	12
5	13	5	13
13	7	13	3

Trace and Write

13 13 13

Thirteen

Thirteen

Paste it

| 5 | 13 | 13 | 9 | 13 | 13 |

Color it

14

Make it

Find and Color

18	13	4	14
9	14	1	14
9	2	14	3

Trace and Write

14 14 14

Fourteen

Fourteen

Paste it

| 17 | 14 | 14 | 7 | 14 | 14 |

Color it

15

Make it

Find and Color

1	5	15	10
15	14	8	15
15	5	11	7

Trace and Write

15 15 15

Fifteen

Fifteen

Paste it

| 15 | 15 | 15 | 15 | 2 | 5 |

Color it

16

Make it

Find and Color

7	4	15	16
16	14	16	15
12	16	11	3

Trace and Write

16 16 16

Sixteen

Sixteen

Paste it

| 11 | 16 | 16 | 8 | 16 | 16 |

17

Color it 17

Make it

Find and Color
5	17	7	17
3	17	11	12
17	4	17	3

✎ **Trace and Write** ✎

17 17 17

Seventeen

Seventeen

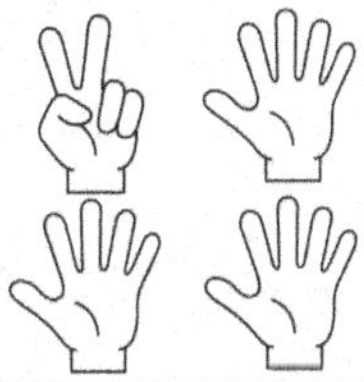

Paste it

| 13 | 17 | 5 | 17 | 17 | 17 |

18

Color it 18

Make it

Find and Color
2	19	18	3
18	13	18	8
1	2	18	7

✎ **Trace and Write** ✎

18 18 18

Eighteen

Eighteen

Paste it

| 18 | 18 | 3 | 18 | 18 | 10 |

19

Color it 19

Make it

Find and Color
8	9	19	9
19	2	19	9
19	5	10	3

✎ **Trace and Write** ✎

19 19 19

Nineteen

Nineteen

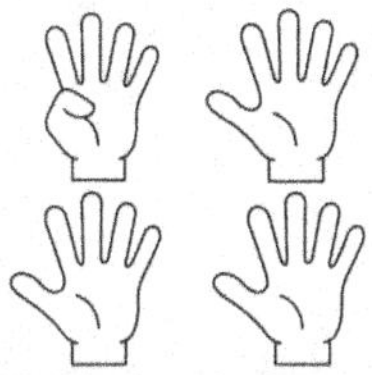

Paste it

| 19 | 19 | 4 | 19 | 1 | 19 |

20

Color it 20

Make it

Find and Color
20	2	10	20
19	3	20	5
20	4	10	20

Trace and Write

20 20 20

Twenty

Twenty

Paste it

| 4 | 20 | 7 | 20 | 20 | 20 |

Which Number is Larger?

Circle the larger number for each pair.

10   5

9   10

3   4

4   8

2   1

7   8

Which Number is Larger?

Circle the larger number for each pair.

Which Number is Smaller?

Circle the smaller number for each pair.

Which Number is Smaller?

Circle the smaller number for each pair.

6 2	8 10
9 7	2 4
6 3	7 4

BIG/small

How many BIG hearts do you see?
Write the answers in the box.

Love Jars
Big/small

How many big hearts?

How many small hearts?

How many total ?

Greater, Equal or Less

Roll 2 dices, write the numbers in the boxes
and write the correct sign in the circle (> = or <).

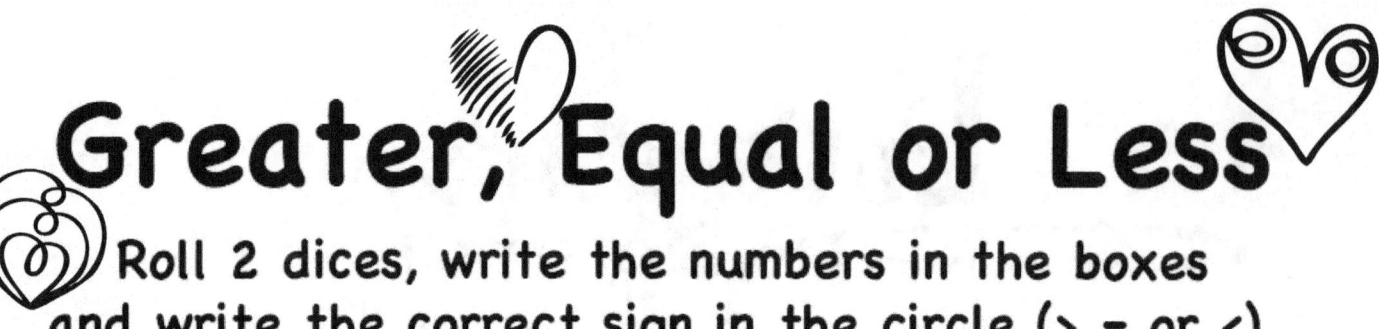

2	<	5

Roll A Value

Roll 2 dices. Draw the value of your dice and
draw your coin to make that amount of
money.

Draw your dice	Value of dice	Draw your coins
	1 3	⑩ ② ①

Subtraction

Roll 2 dices and write the larger number in the 1st box, write the smaller number in the 2nd box and write the answer in the answer box.

5 − 1 = 4   ☐ − ☐ = ☐

☐ − ☐ = ☐   ☐ − ☐ = ☐

☐ − ☐ = ☐   ☐ − ☐ = ☐

☐ − ☐ = ☐   ☐ − ☐ = ☐

☐ − ☐ = ☐   ☐ − ☐ = ☐

☐ − ☐ = ☐   ☐ − ☐ = ☐

Addition

Roll 2 dices, write the numbers in the
first two boxes and write the answer in
the answer box.

$2 + 4 = 6$

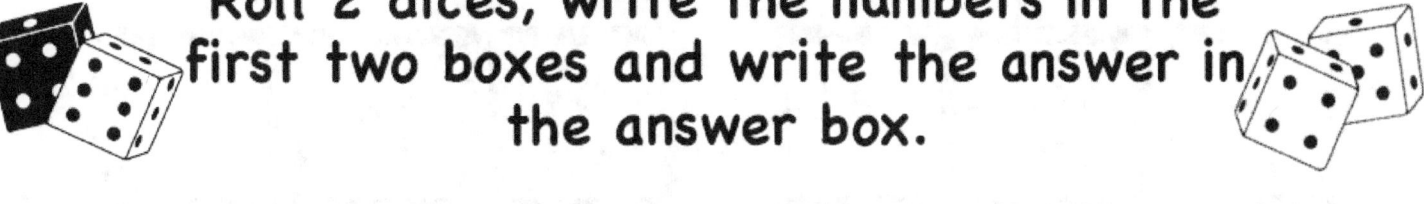

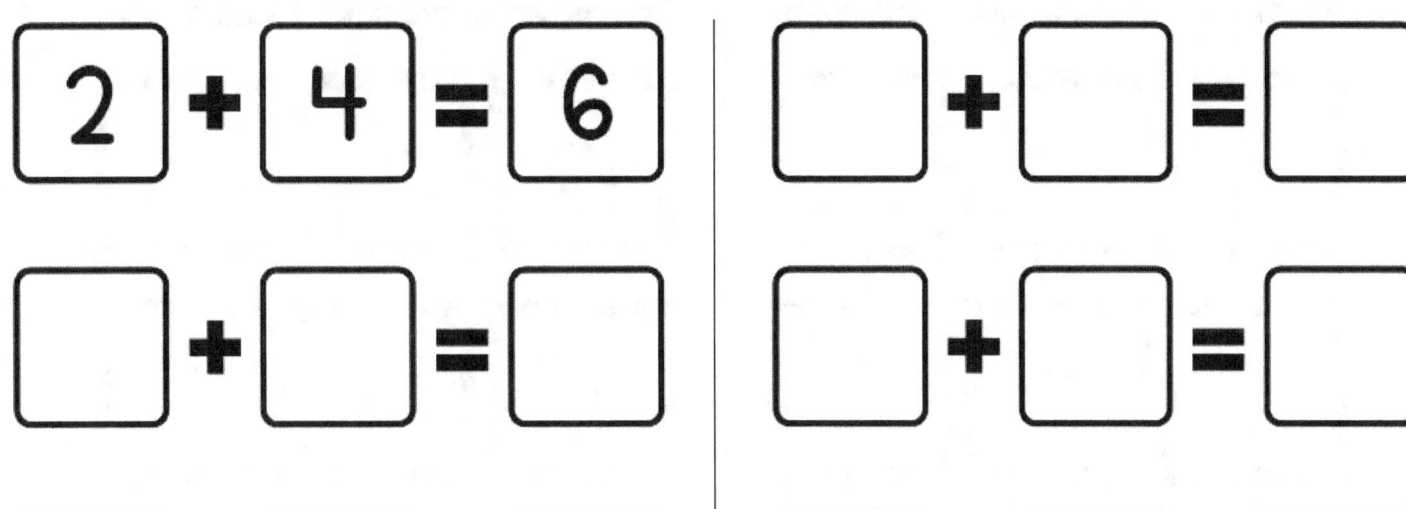

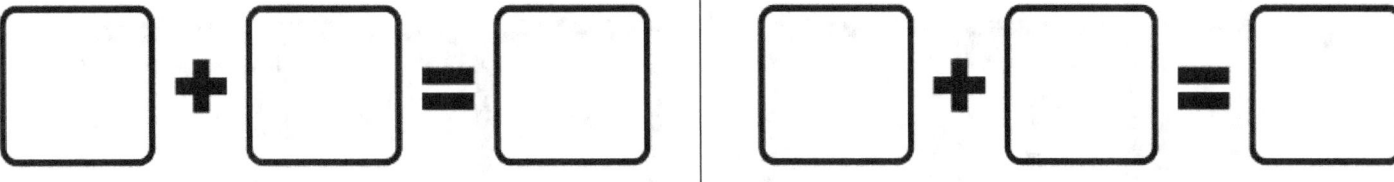

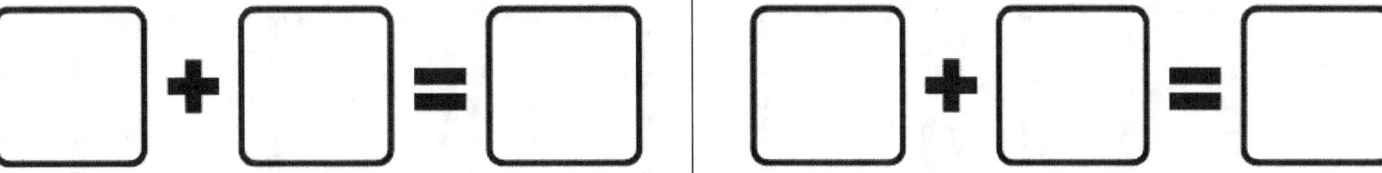

What comes next

Write the number that comes next

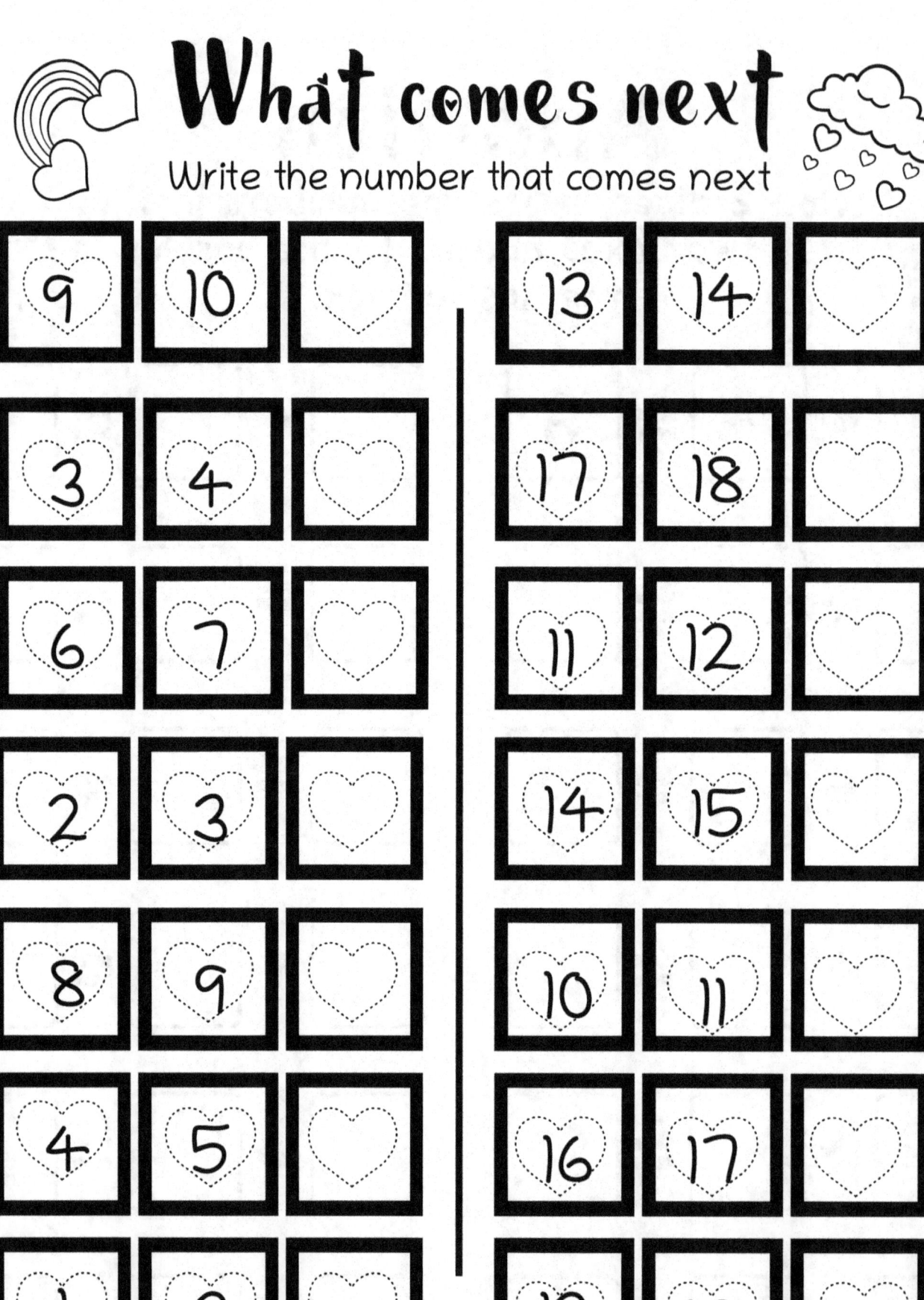

9	10	
3	4	
6	7	
2	3	
8	9	
4	5	
1	2	

13	14	
17	18	
11	12	
14	15	
10	11	
16	17	
12	13	

Let's Count Hearts

How many hearts do you see?

Love

Write the number here:

Counting

How many hearts do you see?
Write the number in the box

How many

Write the number in the box

Love Letter ♥ solve the problem

Write the correct number in the subtraction problem.

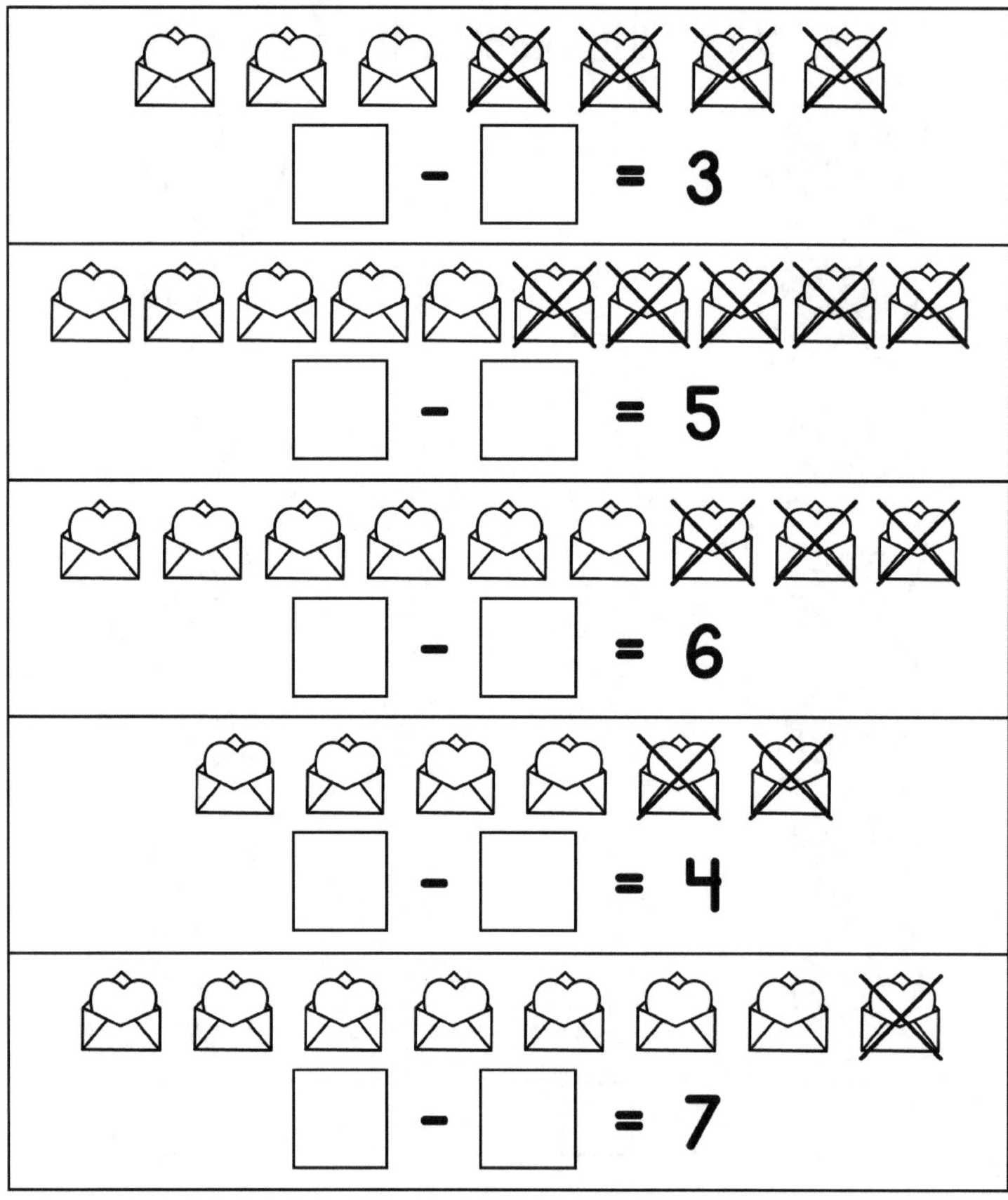

☐ - ☐ = 3

☐ - ☐ = 5

☐ - ☐ = 6

☐ - ☐ = 4

☐ - ☐ = 7

Love Letter ♥ solve the problem

Write the correct number in the subtraction problem.

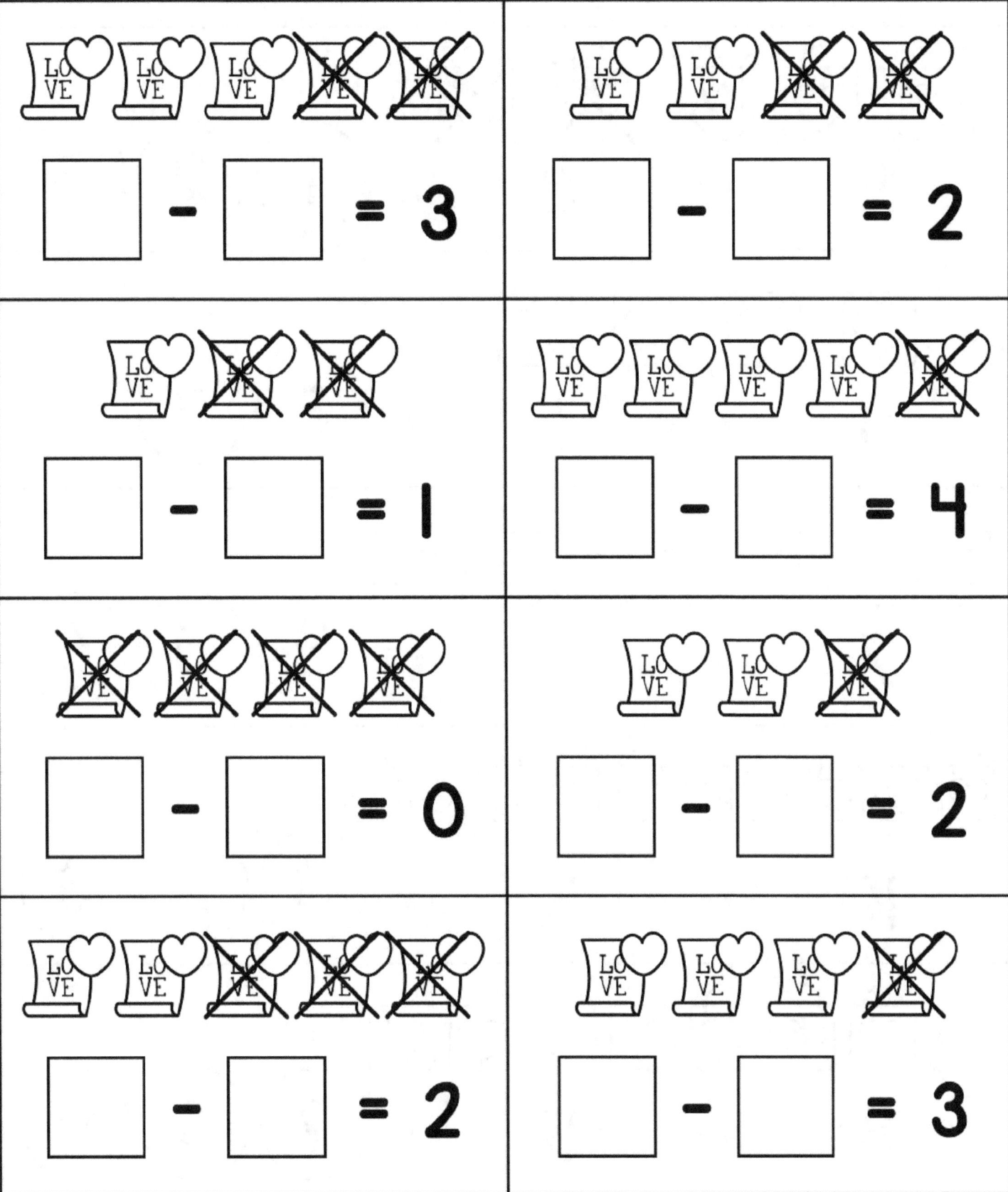

☐ − ☐ = 3

☐ − ☐ = 2

☐ − ☐ = 1

☐ − ☐ = 4

☐ − ☐ = 0

☐ − ☐ = 2

☐ − ☐ = 2

☐ − ☐ = 3

count & subtract ♥ With love

Count the picures, cross out the correct amount and subtract.
Then color the circle that shows the answer.

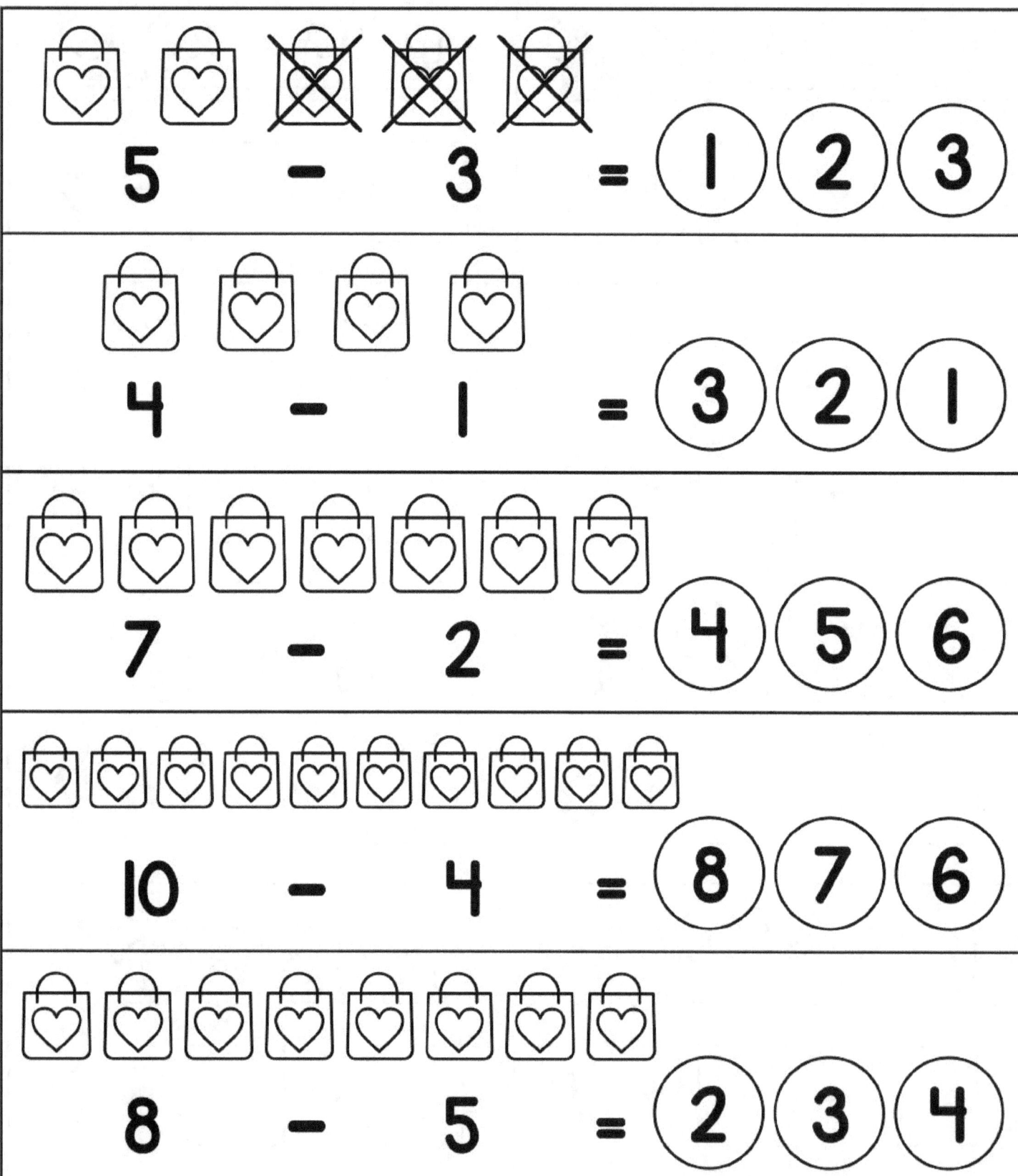

5 − 3 = (1) (2) (3)

4 − 1 = (3) (2) (1)

7 − 2 = (4) (5) (6)

10 − 4 = (8) (7) (6)

8 − 5 = (2) (3) (4)

Valentine's Day ♥ Addition to 5

Solve the addition problems.   Then color the hearts accordingly.

2 + 1 = _____

1 + 3 = _____

2 + 2 = _____

1 + 4 = _____

3 + 2 = _____

1 + 2 = _____

4 + 1 = _____

2 + 3 = _____

3 + 1 = _____

Valentine's Day ♥ Addition to 10

Solve the addition problems.   Then color the hearts accordingly.

$4 + 3 =$ _____   ♡♡♡♡♡♡♡♡♡♡

$5 + 1 =$ _____   ♡♡♡♡♡♡♡♡♡♡

$2 + 7 =$ _____   ♡♡♡♡♡♡♡♡♡♡

$6 + 4 =$ _____   ♡♡♡♡♡♡♡♡♡♡

$2 + 6 =$ _____   ♡♡♡♡♡♡♡♡♡♡

$3 + 4 =$ _____   ♡♡♡♡♡♡♡♡♡♡

$5 + 5 =$ _____   ♡♡♡♡♡♡♡♡♡♡

$6 + 3 =$ _____   ♡♡♡♡♡♡♡♡♡♡

$2 + 8 =$ _____   ♡♡♡♡♡♡♡♡♡♡

Fall in love ♥ counting

Count the pictures to solve the addition problems. Then color the circle that shows the answer.

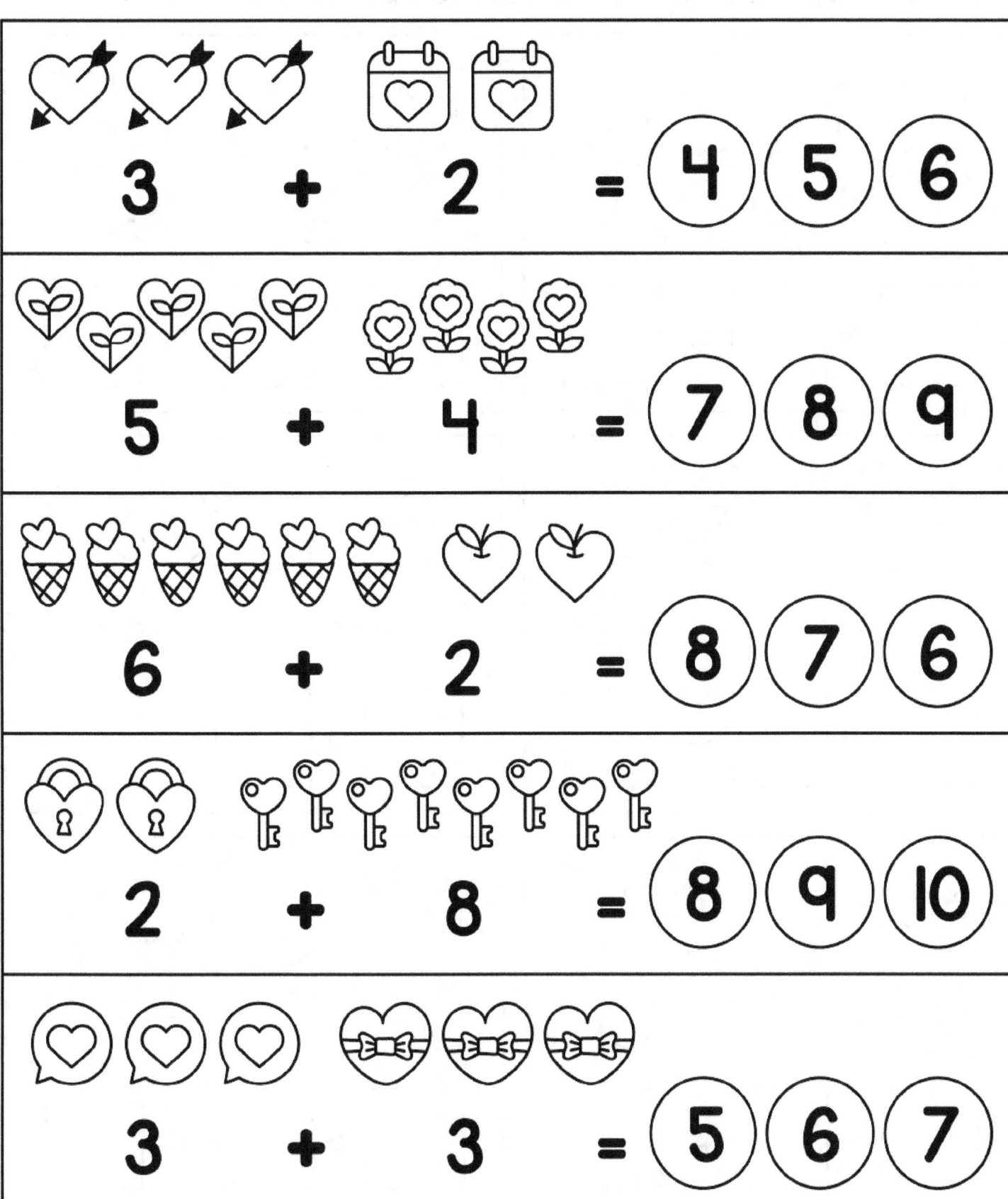

3 + 2 = (4) (5) (6)

5 + 4 = (7) (8) (9)

6 + 2 = (8) (7) (6)

2 + 8 = (8) (9) (10)

3 + 3 = (5) (6) (7)

Full of love ♥ Addition to 5

Count the pictures. Then write the addition problems and solve them.

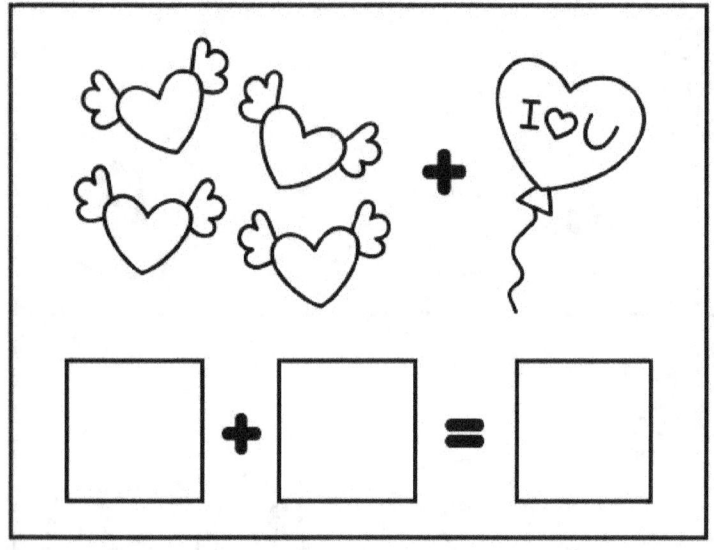

☐ + ☐ = ☐

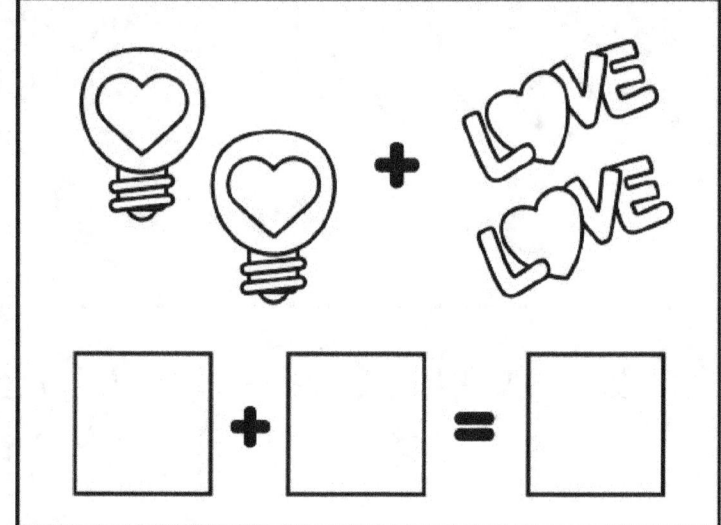

☐ + ☐ = ☐

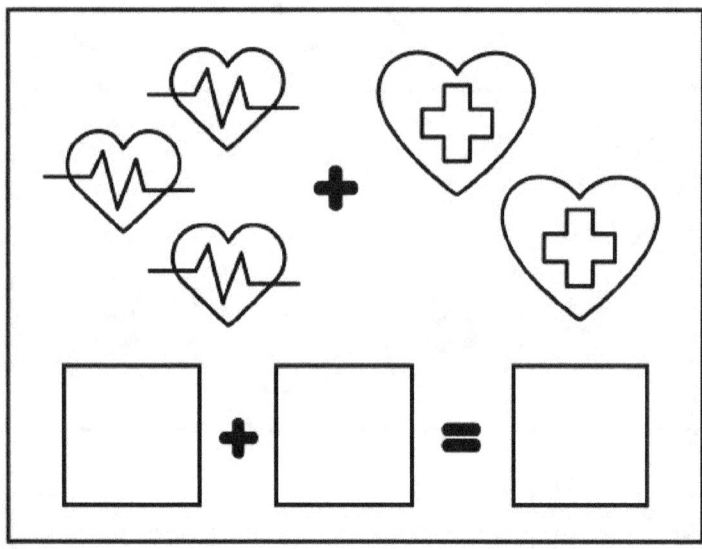

☐ + ☐ = ☐

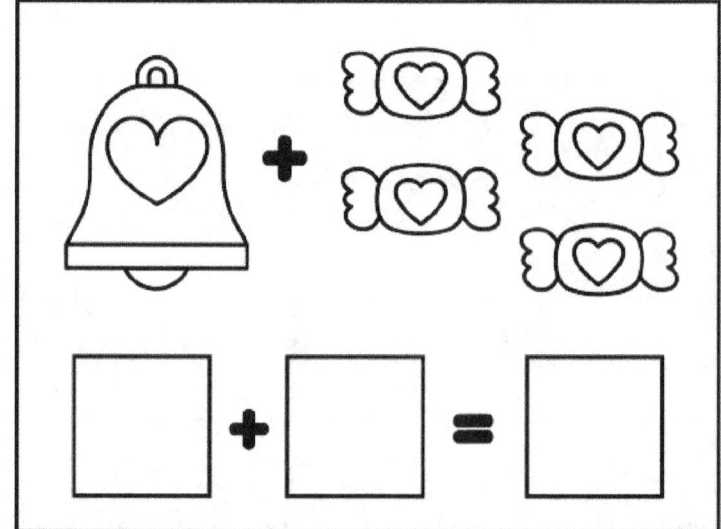

☐ + ☐ = ☐

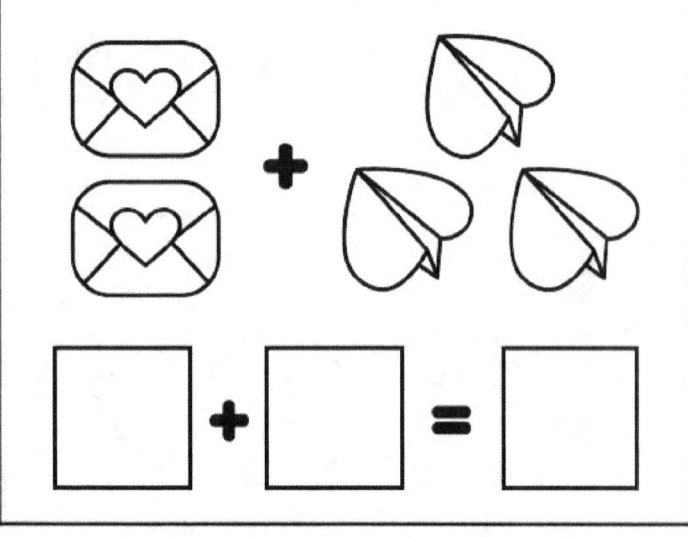

☐ + ☐ = ☐

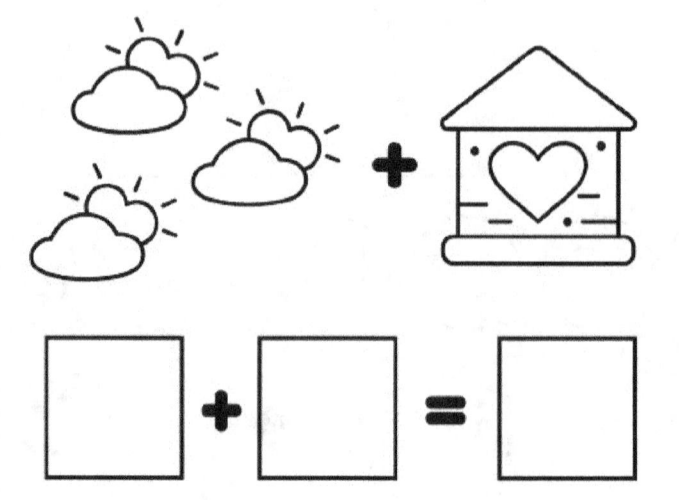

☐ + ☐ = ☐

Full of love ♥ Addition to 5

Count the pictures.   Then write the addition problems and solve them.

☐ + ☐ = ☐

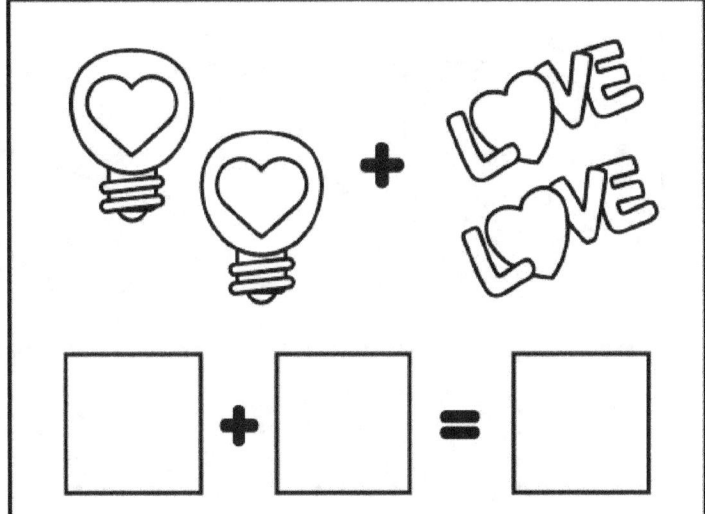

☐ + ☐ = ☐

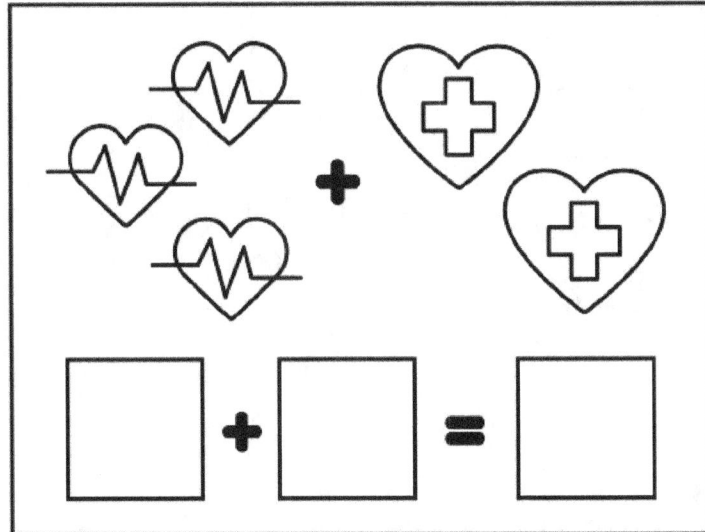

☐ + ☐ = ☐

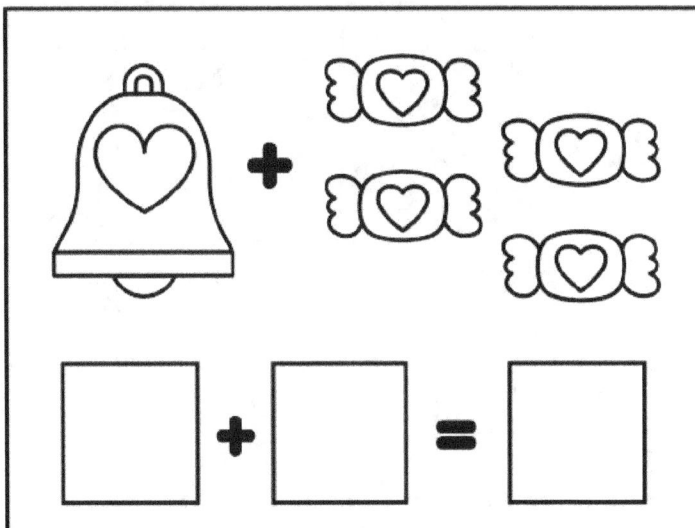

☐ + ☐ = ☐

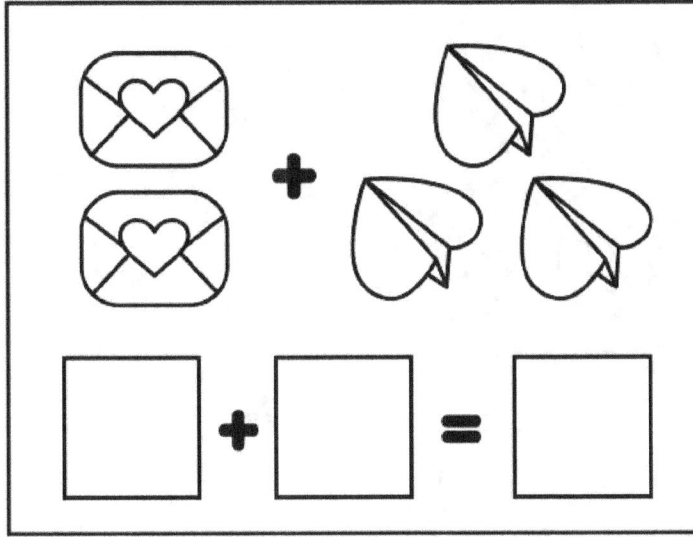

☐ + ☐ = ☐

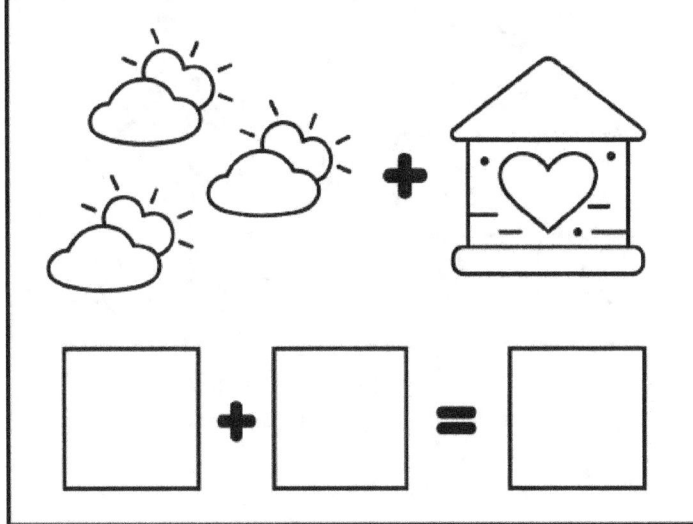

☐ + ☐ = ☐

Full of love ♥ Addition to 10

Count the pictures.   Then write the addition problems and solve them.

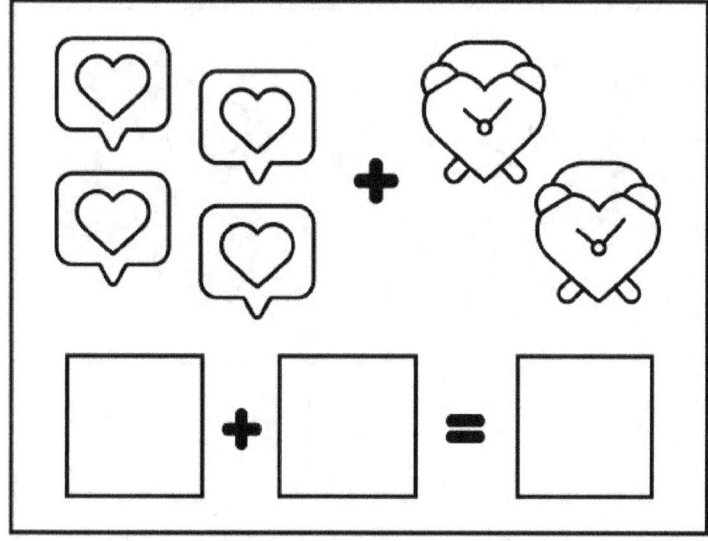

☐ + ☐ = ☐

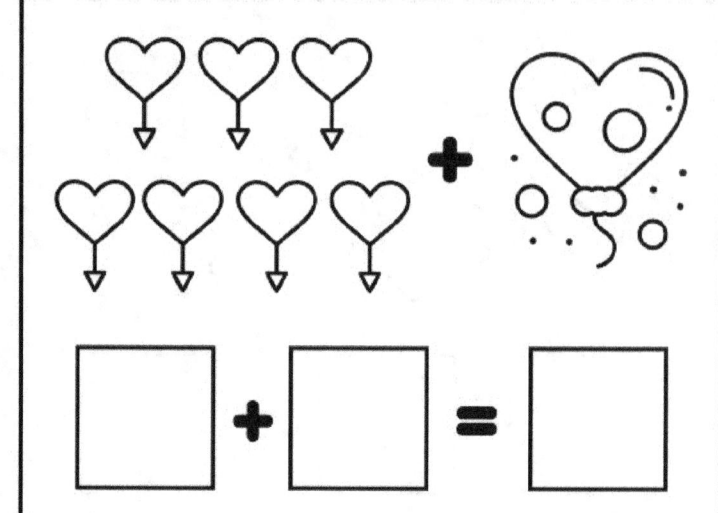

☐ + ☐ = ☐

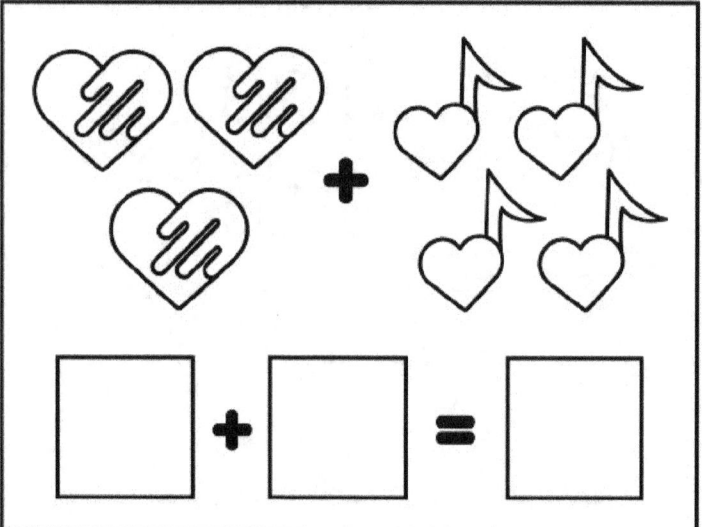

☐ + ☐ = ☐

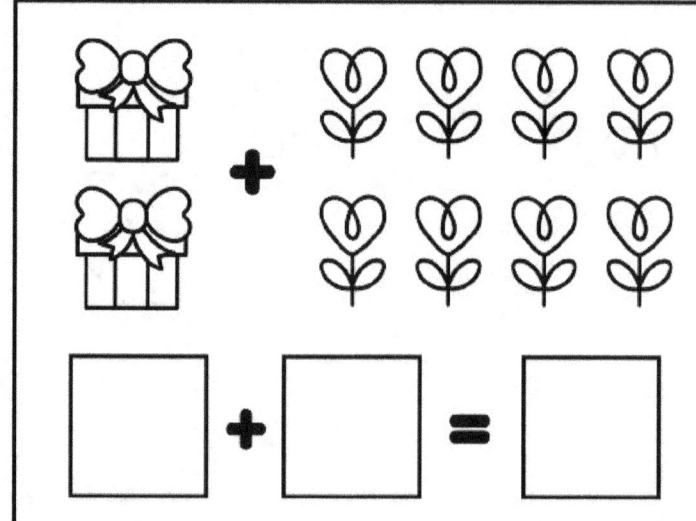

☐ + ☐ = ☐

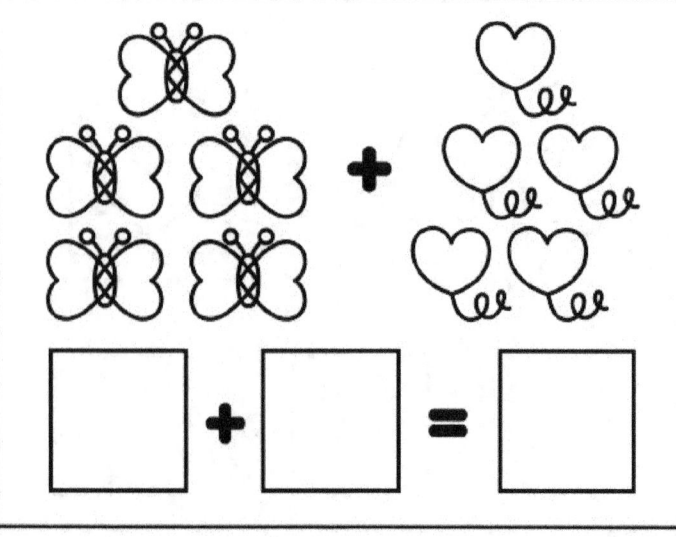

☐ + ☐ = ☐

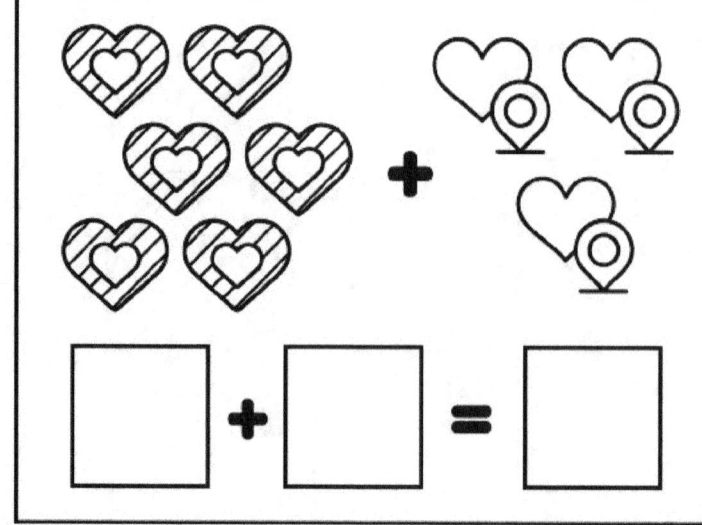

☐ + ☐ = ☐

Cup of love ♥ subtraction below 5

Cross out the pictures to solve the subtraction problems.
Then write the answer.

5 - 1 = _____

4 - 2 = _____

3 - 3 = _____

2 - 1 = _____

4 - 3 = _____

5 - 4 = _____

3 - 1 = _____

2 - 2 = _____

5 - 3 = _____

Sweet heart ♥ subtraction below 10

Cross out the pictures to solve the subtraction problems. Then write the answer.

8 - 4 = _____

6 - 1 = _____

7 - 5 = _____

10 - 3 = _____

9 - 2 = _____

8 - 6 = _____

7 - 1 = _____

6 - 3 = _____

10 - 5 = _____

LOVE i Spy

How many hearts?

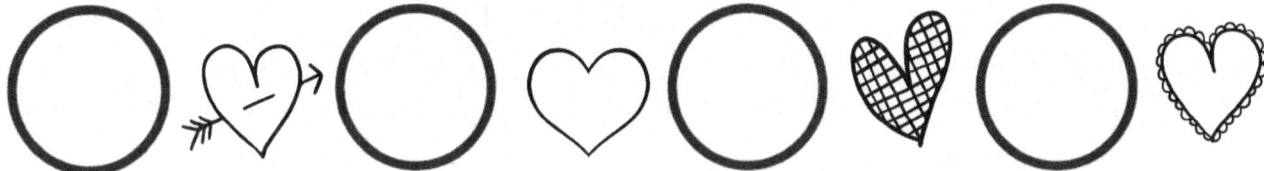

Valentine Maze

Help the kitty to get her cupcake

Trying to find the way

Maze fun

Valentine Gifts

Collect all the gifts

Find something sweet and tasty to eat

Patterns

Write in the box what pattern comes next.

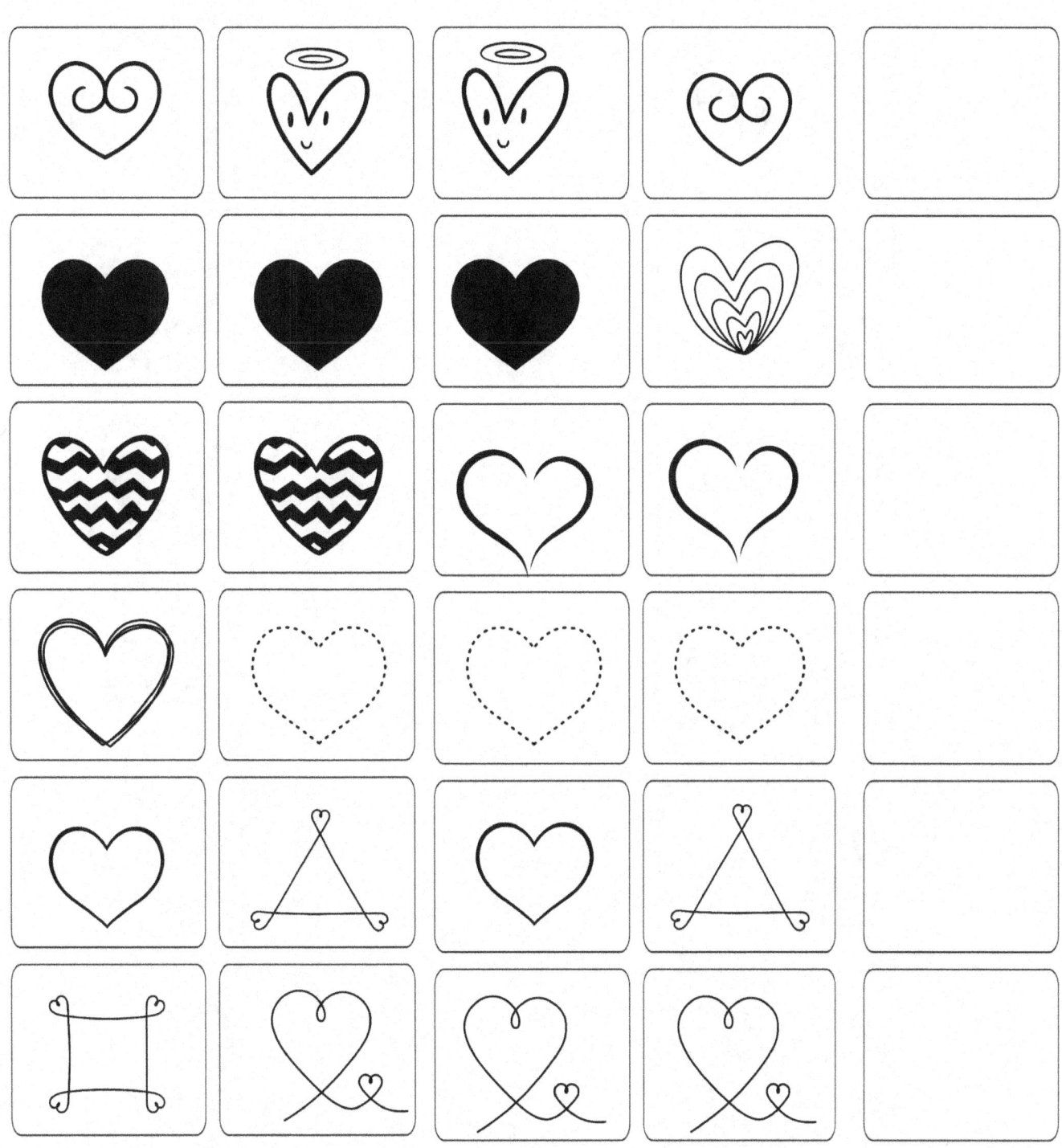

Monster's Heart

Let's help the little monsters to find the right heart

Same or Different
Circle the picture that is different

Same or Different

Circle the pictures that are the same

Spot the differences

Spot the differences

Spot the Differences

How many? 🤍

Connect the Dots

How many? 🤍

SHADOW
MATCHING GAME

FIND THE RIGHT SHADOW

Heart Clock

What time is it?

12:30

9:45

11

1

10

12

2

9

3

8

4

7

5

6

1:00

6:15

Match The Shapes

Draw a line from one shape to the matching shape.

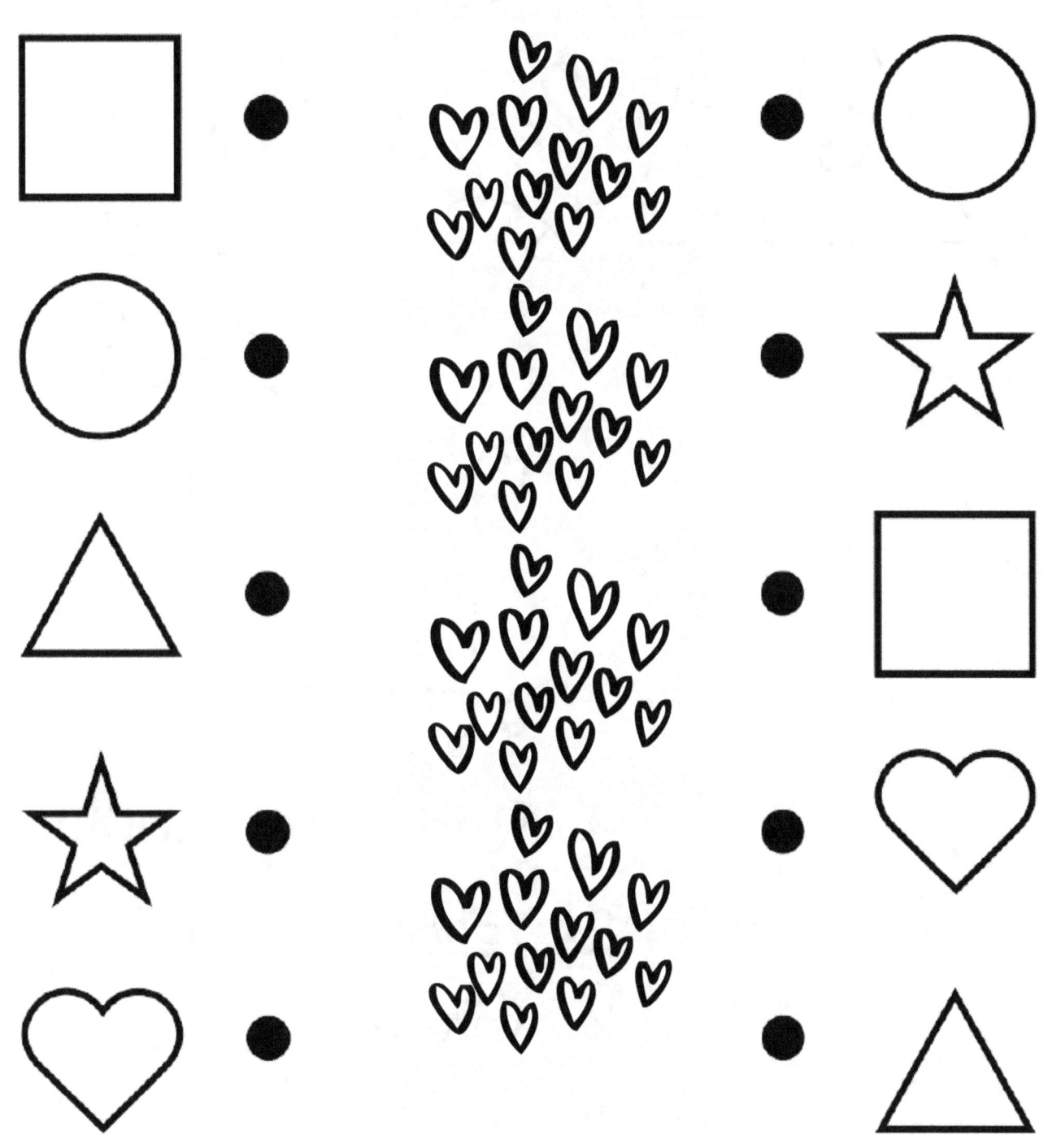

Shapes

Identify the shapes and color by numbers

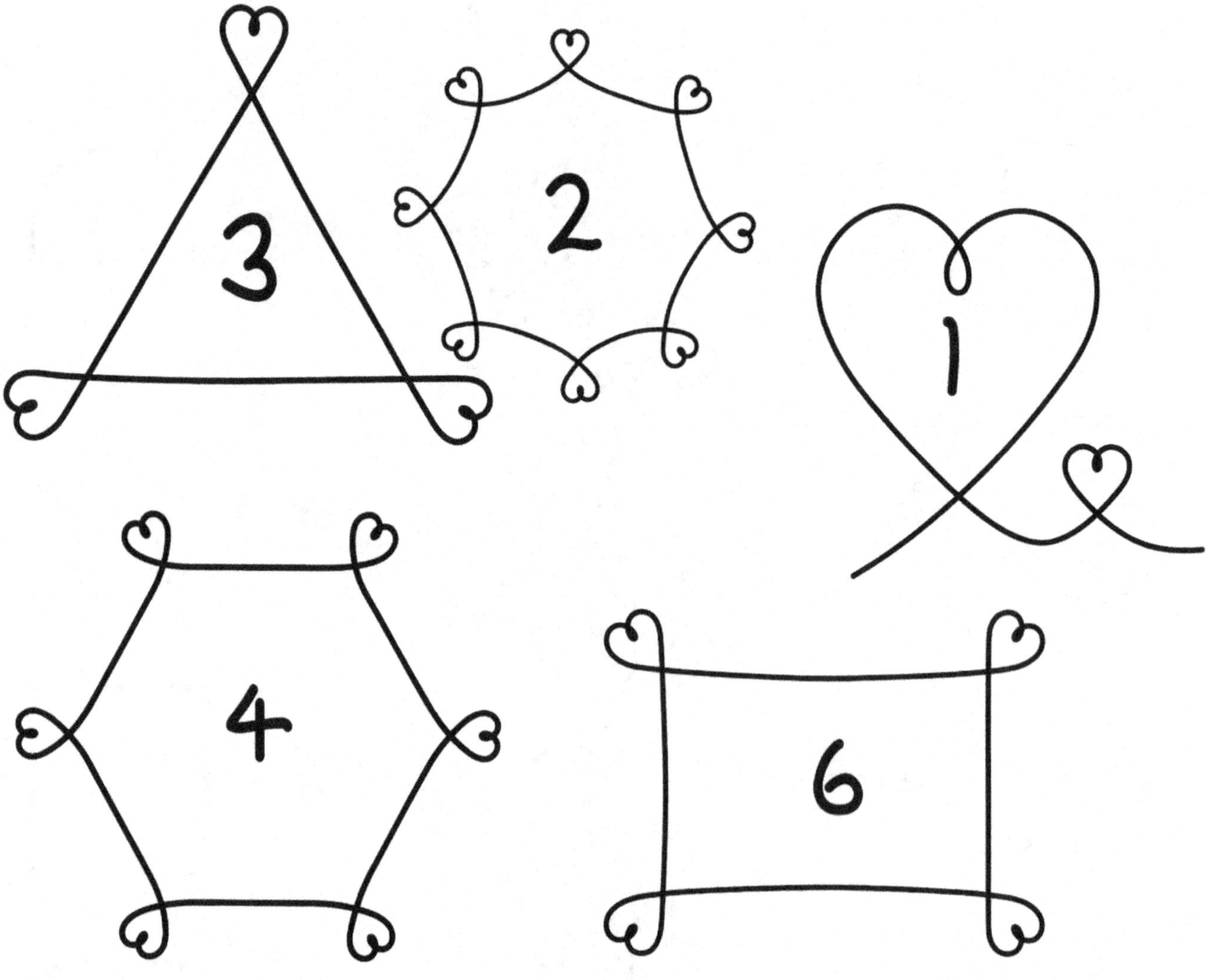

3

2

1

4

6

5

1 - Red   5 - Purple

2 - Yellow   6 - Pink

3 - Green

4 - Blue

Color By Number

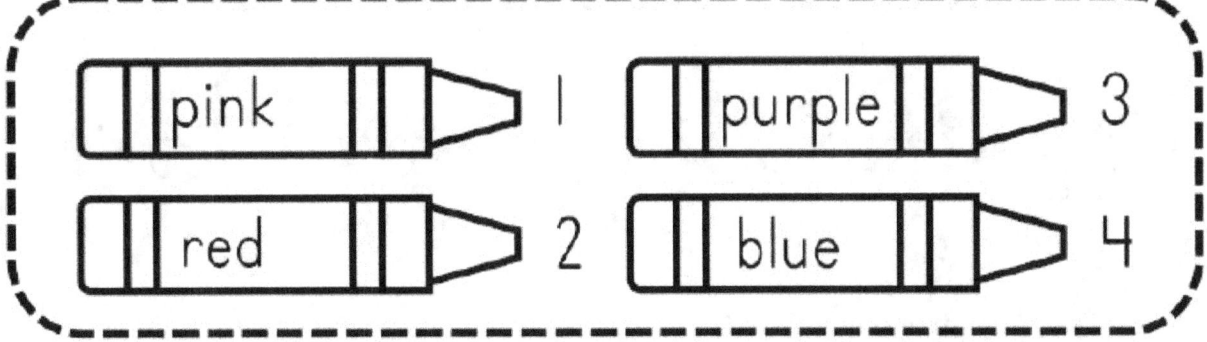

| pink | 1 | purple | 3 |
| red | 2 | blue | 4 |

Color the Picture
Valentine's Day Cup of Love

Tic-Tac-Toe

 # Tic-Tac-Toe

Emotions
How are you feeling today?
Circle the hearts that connect you to that feeling

Draw lovely face

Heart Hug

Name a person you love most. Draw and then color it.